Other books by the same author:

Teaching a Child to Read, University of London Press, 1974.
Psychology Today (ed.), Hodder and Stoughton/TY Books, 1975.
Reconstructing Educational Psychology (ed.), Croom Helm, 1978.

The First Words Language Programme

A Basic Language Programme for Mentally Handicapped Children

BILL GILLHAM

Child Development Research Unit
Department of Psychology
Nottingham University

published jointly by

London
GEORGE ALLEN & UNWIN
Boston   Sydney

and

BEACONSFIELD PUBLISHERS
Beaconsfield

First published in 1979

GEORGE ALLEN & UNWIN LTD
40 Museum Street, London WC1A 1LU

© Bill Gillham, 1979

British Library Cataloguing in Publication Data

Gillham, Bill
   The first words language programme.
   1. Mentally handicapped children—Education
   2. Mentally handicapped children—Language
   3. Speech—Study and teaching
   I. Title
   371.9'28   LC4616   78-40849

   ISBN 0-04-371059-X
   ISBN 0-04-371060-3 Pbk

Typeset in 11 on 13 point Baskerville
and printed in Great Britain
by Biddles Ltd, Guildford, Surrey

This book is dedicated to
JULIE

Preface

This programme is intended for use by parents or teachers with young (probably 3- to 8-year-old) mentally handicapped children who have:

—no 'independent' speech but have imitated some words and show some evidence of understanding language;

OR

—a few 'independent' words (perhaps between ten and twenty) as well as quite a number of imitated words;

OR

—a range of single-word utterances (perhaps as many as fifty or sixty) but still have important gaps in their vocabulary, particularly of those words that go to make up the first sentences.

It is not suitable for children who:

—have not yet reached the mental age level where children usually start to talk (i.e. a mental age of fifteen months plus) which means, in the case of mentally handicapped children, a chronological age of about 2½ years;

—are so deaf that they cannot hear speech accurately even with a hearing aid (many mentally handicapped children have some degree of hearing loss, but hearing for speech is usually adequate);

—are physically incapable of speech.

Briefly, the programme starts by recording what speech (if any) a child already has and then goes on to work out a 'goal' vocabulary based on a study of that particular child and of the words or kinds of words that children have been found to use in their beginning vocabularies.

This 'goal' vocabulary, usually taken ten words at a time, is taught by means of short 'formal' daily sessions of around 10-20 minutes (although less than this to start with) and 'informal' referencing in natural, everyday situations.

The teaching on the programme does not involve working on speech directly (in the sense of just getting the child to 'say the words') but working indirectly by developing and clarifying his *understanding* of language. For real speech is not repeating words after someone else but using them independently, for your own purposes; and this involves having a clear idea of what they mean.

Using this *comprehension* approach the programme takes the child through to the point where he attains his first hundred words — which may well include his first two-word 'sentences'.

It may seem arbitrary to select a hundred words as the limit of the programme. But these first hundred words have a special character — they are not always the ones you might expect — and they cover the stage when language really gets under way. It is also the stage where language appears to be most teachable.

An alternative limit, which may be appropriate with some children, would be the first fifty words since it is from this point that vocabulary growth accelerates very noticeably both in handicapped and non-handicapped children.

There are no miracles in the remediation of mental handicap. The best you can hope for is modest progress from systematic work — which need not be burdensome but does need to be organised.

This manual has been carefully written and compiled: before starting teaching you need to study it equally carefully as well as getting your teaching materials together. Results will vary but at the very least you will be doing something positive and constructive — and many benefits come from that.

Contents

Tables

Acknowledgments

A practical research project carried out over a period of six years means that acknowledgments of help are due to many people.

First, all the children who have been involved in any way with the programme, and their parents; those of my former students who have worked on the programme in schools, in particular Jim Thatcher who carried out the First Hundred Words study of non-handicapped children, and Tony Dessent who took criticism to a new level of candour.

The Nottinghamshire Local Education Authority and notably, Mr. A. G. Croot, Assistant Director for Special Services; the headteachers and staff of Carlton Digby School and the Shepherd School, Nottingham, and Debdale School, Mansfield; Mrs. Dorothy Kabon, Hon. Secretary of the Nottingham and District Association for Mentally Handicapped Children and Adults.

The late Mildred Stevens, formerly Lecturer in Mental Handicap at Matlock College of Education; Rex Brinkworth, Senior Lecturer in Psychology, Birmingham Polytechnic; and Margaret Edwards, Principal Speech Therapist, Nottinghamshire—all of whom read a late draft of the manual and made valuable general and specific criticisms.

Margaret Grainger who has dealt with all the secretarial work relating to the project and has typed many drafts of this manual; Dennis Vardy who made and designed the apparatus and prepared the scale plans; Sam Grainger who has produced the photographic material for the programme and the manual; my research assistant, Paul Livock, who diverted his talents to produce the line drawings and the cover design; and my wife who has helped with the editing, making detailed revisions.

The financial support of the Nuffield Foundation in the development of the programme and the preparation of this manual is gratefully acknowledged.

Chapter 1

Introduction

For the parents and teachers of a mentally handicapped child the time when he starts to speak is probably the most important milestone of all. It is a sign of *real* progress, of a developing intelligence; more than that it means the child and his parents (or his teachers) can be 'in touch' with each other, can communicate with each other, in a way that was not possible before.

It is not surprising, therefore, that parents and teachers make such efforts to get handicapped children to talk. But if this involves concentrating mainly on 'getting him to say the word' then I suspect that the effort is misplaced, because this is not how independent, useful language develops. Clearly a child has to get his words from other people and imitation plays a part in this, but real speech is not just a matter of *saying* the word but also of *understanding* it and its uses. What the child needs to learn are not just words but word meanings; and he needs to learn these words and word meanings so well that when the time comes he can remember them and use them appropriately. The First Words Language Programme is intended to help him to do that.

The nature of the programme

The programme described in this book is distinctive because it is a *language* teaching programme which doesn't focus directly on *speech*—although the development of speech is its aim.

Speech and language are often treated as if they were the same thing, and children are sometimes described as having 'no language' when in fact they may have quite a lot of language (understanding and thinking language) but no speech. There are of course children whose only language problem is a speech problem. But, amongst the mentally handicapped, there are certainly many children whose slow speech development is due largely to their failure to make progress at those stages of language development that come *before* speech—in particular that stage where children show by their increasing comprehension that they are taking language in, even though they are not actually saying very much.

Severe speech problems require the specialist help of a speech therapist but working on the understanding of language—and encouraging independent speech—is something we can all do provided we have a sensible plan of action, the necessary practical ideas and materials, and the co-operation of the child.

1

The development of language

We still have much to learn about the growth of language in young and mentally handicapped children, but what is clear is that much progress is made in language development before any independent speech appears. Speech is the end of a long process and has its roots in the pre-verbal patterns of communication that are developed between the baby and his parents—particularly his mother. This experience of communication is basic to the social uses of the vocabulary he will soon start to acquire; equally basic is the baby's pre-verbal knowledge of his world. On both counts the foundation of speech is laid down before language comes on the scene at all. Before babies can speak, or understand what is said to them, they spend much of their time learning and making sense of what people mean and what is going on around them. This knowledge will later form the basis for the word meanings a child develops—in conjunction with how he observes adults use these words.

The link between language and pre-verbal communication is seen most clearly in the baby's attempts to imitate. *Imitation* of sounds and actions is one of the ways in which the baby gets in touch with people and so it is not surprising that, early on, he tries to imitate speech. In non-handicapped children this usually occurs at around ten to thirteen months and in a sense is a 'false start' in language because it looks like the beginning of real speech but isn't. It is closely followed by increasing evidence of language comprehension and then, often quite quickly, independent speech gets under way. The period between 'imitated' speech and 'independent' speech—when language seems to have gone underground—is longer in handicapped children and their parents sometimes think that they have 'lost' what language they had. But in fact they may have gone on to the more important stage of comprehension; and it is at this 'input' level that language teaching seems to have the greatest chance of being effective.

'But he understands everything you say . . .'

Sometimes this is true to the extent that the child *would* say the words if he (physically) could. But it is more likely to be half-true in a way which involves a rather subtle distinction: the difference between understanding language sufficiently to understand what people mean and understanding language well enough to speak it.

If you are learning a foreign language you will quite soon reach the level where you can get the gist of what people are saying; but it will be some time before you are able to remember the words you have heard well enough to use them to *speak* in that language. Going back a step, when you are at the stage of trying to understand what is being said in the unfamiliar language you will find yourself paying attention to anything in the situation that might give you a clue as to what is meant: as a result you may appear to understand more than you do. In this respect your experience is something like the mentally handicapped child at the beginning of language.

What looks like language comprehension in the young handicapped child is often more a matter of understanding and using all the non-language information available. Remember that from an early age children are having to make sense of the world — including what people are trying to communicate — long before they have any language skill to help them. For all children non-language communication comes first. The child with language delay has almost certainly learnt to use all the non-linguistic cues as to what people mean — the familiar routine, gesture accompanying speech, tone of voice, facial expression, what other people are doing, and so on. Because we, as adults, pay special attention to what people say — and act accordingly — it is easy to assume that when a child does what we have told him to do, it is because he has understood *the words* we have used.

However, when all the non-linguistic cues are deleted (as in the Level Two choice discrimination tasks — see page 17) the results can be surprising even to people who know the child well.

Selecting children for the programme

Even the most successful teaching of mentally handicapped children takes a great deal of time and effort. Since the present programme is not appropriate for all such children it is important to identify those children for whom it is unlikely to work. Most of the categories are obvious ones.

1. *Children who have not yet reached the mental age level where children usually start to talk.* Mentally handicapped children are, by definition, slower in their rate of intellectual development than other children: it seems unlikely that they will be able to benefit from a systematic language remediation programme until they have reached a mental age level of around 15 to 24 months. The problem is getting good evidence to judge children on: often they do not show what they can do on a formal intelligence test. The best evidence usually comes from asking parents and teachers (or parents and teachers asking themselves) what their child can do, and observing the child in play. But what are you looking for? Very simply you are looking for evidence that what the child does is under the control of what goes on inside his head. The more he shows that he has plans and ideas of his own, the more sure you can be that he has the kind of knowledge that language can build on. So, you look to see if he searches for things that are out of sight — which shows that he has the *idea* of it in his mind; to see if he recognises objects and toys that are not quite the same as the ones he is

familiar with, showing that he knows what to do with them — for example, setting out toy cups and saucers; to see if he engages in any 'pretend' play like pushing a toy car (or a wooden block) around the floor and making car noises, or 'hoovering' the carpet with a stick; and you watch for evidence of imitation, copying what somebody else has just been doing with a toy, like crashing two cars together or trying to balance one block on top of another.

In the end you may have only a provisional judgment: in such marginal cases the only sensible assessment that remains is trial teaching — trying to teach word meanings and seeing what happens.

2. *Children who do not have adequate hearing for speech.* Many mentally handicapped children have some degree of hearing loss but it is often of no great practical significance. However, *any* child with language delay should have a question mark against his hearing until a satisfactory assessment has been carried out. Fortunately this is now standard practice and only rarely is information not available, although a number of children whose records show that their hearing has been 'tested' may well be down for a re-test because of the audiologist's doubts about the results: it is always best to check the original report.

3. *Children who are physically incapable of speech.* This is a difficult category to identify and one of the most frustrating to encounter. If the problem seems to be at the level of the control of the organs of speech then the opinion of a speech therapist can be valuable. She may be able to say that control of the breath, lips and tongue is improving and that speech is a 'possible'. But the defect may be more fundamental and inaccessible than that. The best check is to see whether the child has *ever* imitated speech; if he is physically capable of imitating speech — if he can say words whether he understands them or not — then there are no *physical* barriers to independent speech.

Assessing children for the programme

To recap, the programme is intended for: children who have imitated speech and show signs of understanding language, but have not yet developed independent speech themselves; children who have a small number of words of their own (perhaps ten or twenty); children who have a fair number of single words (perhaps as many as sixty) but still have important gaps in their vocabulary.

Deciding into which of these three groups a particular child falls is not difficult, but it is important not to make a hasty judgment of what speech a child has on the basis of a general impression: precise information is needed.

The first question to ask is: what words does he already have? And, in particular, what *imitated* words does he have and what *independent* words does he have? This is not as simple to answer as it appears, even if you are the child's parent. What usually happens is that when you make a systematic attempt to write down all the words your child says you find that he can say more than you realised; and there may be some words you are not sure about that you will need to check on by watching and listening more carefully.

This record has to be accurate because you need to know where to start — which means knowing what you began with and what you don't have to teach. However, a simple list of the words a child uses will not, on its own, give you enough insight into what he can do and how he is progressing. You need to have a note of what was going on, what he seemed to be trying to convey when he used the word, and whether he went on to use it regularly.

If the child attends school then it is useful to have a record of words used at home and also a record of those used at school (e.g. through a home-and-school diary). Our experience is that there are substantial similarities but some differences — words that are used in one setting but not in the other: it might be worthwhile to try to 'transfer' these words to the other setting.

In Appendix A there are examples of special forms for keeping these records, and guidance on how to use them. There are three different forms, for imitated speech (words and phrases), for independent words, and for sentences. Examples of how these are filled in are given on page 6.

It is important to distinguish between 'imitated' words and 'independent' words. In a sense all words are imitated — the child doesn't invent them; they are all learnt because he's heard somebody use them. It's *how* he uses them that makes the difference. If he uses them for his own purposes, to say what *he* wants to say then they are *his* independent words: he has reached the stage of useful language. But the child who has reached the stage where he repeats words that other people say has also passed an important milestone in his development: at the very least imitation means that the child is taking notice of speech and is capable of speaking. It also usually means that independent speech is not far away, and the first 'independent' words often include some of the words he has been known to imitate.

Independent words are of two kinds — 'private' and 'public'. Private words are those where the child knows what he means and so do people in his family — and perhaps some neighbours and friends. Public words are those that (almost) anybody can understand, although they may not be said very clearly — or even very completely (e.g. 'mi' for 'milk'). Public words are more useful, but both kinds are real words that the child uses for his own purposes: they are equally a sign of progress.

Any new words appearing in sentences (i.e. that haven't appeared before as single words) go on the 'independent' word sheets. Most of the early two-word sentences consist of one word that appears quite often (e.g. 'gone') and another word that varies. Each new combination is recorded ('car gone', 'dolly gone', 'sweetie gone') since this is an important aspect of progress. Sometimes two words are so run together that it is clear the child is using them as one word (e.g. 'allgone'): these are treated as single words.

Table 1.1   *Examples of Completed Record Forms*

'IMITATED' SPEECH RECORD

Word or phrase	Date first imitated	Who said the word or phrase that was imitated	What was going on?	Why do you think he imitated what was said?
cack-cack (or something like that!)	1/7/77	mother	looking at picture of duck in a book	? because mother emphasised it

'INDEPENDENT' WORD RECORD

'Public' or 'private' word	Date first used	To whom (or to what) was the word said?	What was going on?	What do you think he was trying to say?	Was it used again fairly frequently?
eyes	5/4/78	to mother	talking face to face - pointed at eyes	there are your eyes	? yes

SENTENCE RECORD

Sentence	Date first used	To whom or what used?	What was going on?	What do you think he was trying to say?	Was it used again fairly frequently?
Daddy coat	4/10/78	to mother	saw father's coat hanging on peg	that's daddy's coat	yes

Deciding what words to teach

Having worked out what words a child already has you are in a position to decide what words you should try to teach him. This is not as easy as it sounds and was one of the major difficulties encountered in developing this programme. Initially we did not expect that specifying the words you should teach a child would present any real problems. Like most people we thought we knew what words would be most useful for a beginning vocabulary. However, even though we took into account the children's circumstances and apparent interests, we began to doubt whether the words being taught (colour names, for instance) were really the ones they would want to use in the early stages of independent speech. Our goal words were largely the result of adult conjecture. It took us some time to formulate what now seems the simple and obvious question, namely: *what are the first words children use when they start to talk?*

We went on to study the early vocabulary of a sample of fourteen babies, getting their mothers to record the first hundred words their babies produced as they emerged in the course of development. We also looked at an American study (Nelson, 1973) which had followed up nineteen babies for their first fifty words. We were impressed by the similarity of the vocabulary of the American babies and those in our study. In particular, we found that our 'high frequency' words were almost identical with the 'high frequency' words in the American study — which suggested that they might represent a necessary core vocabulary for teaching language-delayed children. Obviously some words were only used by one child, but most impressive was the extent to which children brought up in different homes and different countries used the *same* words and talked about the same things. We have subsequently carried out a study of the first fifty words produced by four Down's children (not amongst those we have taught), which indicates that in terms of what they want to talk about, Down's children do not seem to differ from others.

This research has enabled us to produce the lists of the words that appeared most frequently (Appendix E) and the developmental vocabulary lists on pages 8 and 9. These lists are based on the vocabulary records of the fourteen non-handicapped babies, and the developmental lists present the words in the order in which they appeared.

A 'goal' vocabulary is worked out by selecting words from these developmental lists *taking into account the individual characteristics of the child in question*. What is *he* interested in? What are the words *he* is likely to use, and so on. The developmental lists are intended to guide your choice but can, of course, be supplemented by other words likely to have 'talk' value. The names of the 'important' people (or animals) in a child's life are the most obvious but there are sometimes special circumstances or interests (e.g. the little boy living near an RAF airfield whose first word was "copter").

The words are divided into those that occurred most commonly at each ten-word stage (e.g. from the 11th to the 20th word). There are *thirty* words at each of these stages which are divided into three groups of ten, the first ten being those that occurred most frequently at that stage, and so on. There are rather less than 300 words altogether because sometimes the same word was produced earlier (or later) by some of the children. Overall the fourteen babies we studied produced a total of 383 different words — excluding people's names — but some of the words were only used by one child.

Table 1.2 *Developmental Vocabulary Lists (The First Hundred Words)*

You will see that some words occur more than once:
this is because they were common at more than one stage.

Stage	Frequency + + +		Frequency + +		Sentence words +	
One 1st — 10th words	daddy car *dog baby bye-bye	mummy (person's name) *teddy *cat ta	gone ball *bird tree *horse	(*drink) no biscuit shoe there	hello banana spoon bubbles *clock	sock bus bang nose key
Two 11th — 20th words	shoe *dog ball book hello	*duck baby door *horse *bird	*clock down no bye-bye pretty	car me train bath *teddy	fish allgone flower *cow teeth	cup bag bus tree ear
Three 21st — 30th words	(person's name) down *bird chair bye-bye	eye nose boat more button	*duck gone hair key shoe	door hot jelly paper spoon	teeth tap again blanket man	swing van balloon juice seesaw
Four 31st — 40th words	(person's name) ball book eye tea	bath *bird *cat knee baby	bye-bye bus chair cheese hair	bang *cow *clock ear hand	stairs where lorry lolly tractor	toe oh dear look pram potty

* Various ways of saying the word.

Stage	Frequency +++		Frequency ++		Frequency +		Sentence words
Five 41st — 50th words	(person's name) door balloon peas brush	bike bed hair book bad	coat ear hot oh dear spoon	drawer here y'are milk plane train	blow clap fly orange more	brick fish here kick purse	
Six 51st — 60th words	(person's name) *clock on pear bin	biscuit bricks pen back boat	bath bunny dirty knee purse	bag *cat key mine toe	bridge again here my peg	what fork more pull apple	where + TOPIC** there + TOPIC here + TOPIC it's + TOPIC my + TOPIC TOPIC + on
Seven 61st — 70th words	(person's name) cake up bunny bread	toast where brush bag donkey	dinner hot oh dear scissors walk	fork night-night pin sock beans	carry chocolate gun mess open	cold *boy knife nasty watch	TOPIC + gone hello + PERSON/ANIMAL more + TOPIC bye-bye + PERSON/ANIMAL PERSON/ANIMAL + come open + TOPIC

Eight 71st — 80th words	(person's name) doll egg hand juice	*cow bottle home hole mouse	mess out peg peas go	night-night potatoes pin sit gate	bang down meat knock-knock laces	cry dance hat push water	sit (down) + PERSON/ANIMAL
							 PERSON/ANIMAL + down
							 TOPIC + PERSON/ANIMAL
							   e.g. toast Mummy
							   (possessive)

Nine 81st — 90th words	(person's name) seesaw bath coat fish	hat bang big *dog juice	my more peg spoon tap	milkman oh dear pudding tea teeth	bowl here kick please spade	brush hot nice shut splash	TOPIC + †back big + TOPIC in + TOPIC this + TOPIC got + TOPIC shut + TOPIC
Ten 91st — 100th words	(person's name) dig fly (flies) sit train	book house mouse towel walk	garden light outside there window	horse noise road water again	boots big come kiss scissors	bounce broken jump moon pop	allgone + TOPIC up + TOPIC look + TOPIC TOPIC + ACTION (e.g. boy jump)

* Various ways of saying the word.

** TOPICS are the names of things (or people or animals) e.g. 'where daddy', 'my apple'.

† Usually meaning place, e.g. 'mummy back' (of car) or movement, e.g. 'train back'.

You start from the vocabulary stage the child you are working with has already reached: obviously there is no need to concentrate on the first ten words with a child who has thirty or forty independent words. You select your goal vocabulary to work on five to ten words at a time; in practice we have found this just about the right number — enough to give variety but not so many that you can't keep in mind exactly what words you're aiming for.

With the child who has no independent speech your first group of goal words is worked out on the basis of the first words that children have been found to produce in speech. It would be naïve to assume that you can make up a child's mind for him as to exactly what these words will be, but at this stage children have more words (or kinds of words) in common than they ever will again* so it is possible to make a very good guess — and then make these words *available* to the child.

Making words available to a child is what the programme is about: it is not an attempt to determine absolutely what words a child will speak, but to put in his way words he might want to speak.

In the case of the child who already has a number of words of his own — be it ten or fifty — the 'goal' vocabulary needs to be selected from the stage he has reached. For example, if he has twenty words then you select your 'goal' words from the third stage (words occurring between the 21st and 30th). If you wish you can also select a 'control' group of words *that you don't teach* — the purpose of this is explained below.

If a child is in the middle of a ten-word stage then it is probably sensible to choose words only from that level, but it is a matter of judgment. It may make more sense to combine a few words from that stage with some from the next.

The child who has a fair number of single words — fifty or sixty — needs further work on his vocabulary, in particular those words which go to make up the first sentences. Two-word sentences usually start to appear at about the fifty word stage in non-handicapped children, but in handicapped children the one-word stage is often longer. Teaching children how to put words together will be the subject of a later book but in the present programme it seems worthwhile to try and teach the commonest 'sentence words' (like 'gone' and 'more'). These sentence words are shown at the vocabulary stage where they first appear in sentences — they have usually appeared earlier as single words.

Evaluating the effects of your teaching (goal and control words)

There are four main problems in developing a language programme like the present one. Firstly, working out an adequate theoretical basis (which beyond a certain point doesn't interest everyone: it is summarised in Appendix B). Secondly, working out exactly what it is you want to teach. Thirdly, developing materials and techniques for actually doing the teaching. And finally, devising a

*See page 73.

way of finding out whether this teaching is having any real effect. Not everyone feels the need to 'evaluate' what they are doing, but if you are working on a child's language you will almost certainly observe changes—more words will appear in speech, including the ones you are working on. But perhaps the child would have produced them anyway? What can look like the results of special help may be nothing of the sort.

One of the ways in which psychologists evaluate the effects of different types of teaching or training on people is to have a 'control' group and an 'experimental' group. The experimental group gets the special teaching or training, the control group gets nothing or something different. Any difference in results is assumed to be due to the different treatment the two groups received.

But there are difficulties in applying this procedure to the mentally handicapped. Firstly there are not very large numbers of these children—and they are often highly individual: getting two matched groups of reasonable size is almost impossible. Secondly, the idea of selecting two groups of handicapped children, giving one group special help and giving the other group nothing extra or something you don't believe in, is ethically unacceptable to most research workers, parents and teachers. And yet evaluation is important to all of them. Does the programme work? Is it having any effect?

We finally devised a technique which enabled us to evaluate the programme and which can also be used by parents or teachers working with an individual child. It consists of having an experimental group and a control group, made up not of children you teach and children you don't, but of *words* that you teach (or don't teach)—*goal* words and *control* words.

To do this you select *pairs* of words of equal frequency from the vocabulary list. From each pair one word is assigned to the 'goal' group (i.e. the words that will be taught) and the other to the 'control' group (i.e. the words that will *not* be taught). Of course this doesn't mean that you avoid using the 'control' words in the normal way—you just don't deliberately teach them.

If teaching has no effect then words from the 'goal' group and the 'control' group have an equal chance of appearing in speech. If the goal words appear more often than one would expect by chance then it is reasonable to think that teaching is doing something. An illustration of how this works out in practice as well as the statistical technique for working out whether a difference is really significant are given in Appendix C.

One aspect of evaluation is to judge the size of your contribution to the child's language; the effort is probably only worthwhile if the words taught make up a significant proportion of the new words the child adds to his vocabulary. If the goal words make up much less than a quarter of *all* new independent words then the programme may be superfluous—I say 'may be' because I have reason to believe that the structured approach of the programme *encourages a general growth in vocabulary*. I think this is especially true after the first ten-word stage.

All new words are recorded on the same forms that were used to assess what speech the child started with. You also need to record on the forms the point at which you begin teaching each group of goal words (e.g. 'First group of goal words started here').

Remember that the progress that counts is not in terms of the words a child imitates or words that are forced out of him by getting him to name things ('What's that?', 'What's that?' and so on). The words you look for are the ones he produces *independently*, without prompting. The interest lies in seeing whether these are the ones you have taught him!

Chapter 2

Organising the Teaching

The approach outlined in the introductory chapter might look as if it presumed to be all that is necessary to develop language in mentally handicapped children. In fact, at most it can only be a small part in the process but, hopefully, a significant one—what one might call the *deliberate element*. Most children learn to speak without anyone teaching them but mentally handicapped children often benefit from special help.

I don't think anyone has ever managed to put successful teaching down on paper: in the end it depends on the personalities of the people involved. But if you can't specify these subtleties or exactly how you get on with a particular child, it is possible to say how you can organise your deliberate teaching, and what methods and materials you use. And then leave people to handle the subtleties for themselves—which they would do anyway.

So although you can't put down everything that makes for successful teaching you can indicate some of its essential ingredients. In broad terms these are:

clear *objectives*: knowing what it is you want the child to learn;
good *organisation*: knowing how you are going to teach what you want the child to learn—and having alternative techniques and materials available;
accurate *feedback*: knowing what progress the child is making—this may well be slow, but precise records mean that you won't lose track—or lose heart!

The first and last of these we have already dealt with; the rest of this book is devoted to the second one, the essentially practical aspects of the programme.

The teaching plan

There are three fundamentals to the organisation of teaching:

a good range of teaching materials particularly different ways of teaching the same thing: mentally handicapped children differ very much as to what they will work for as well as how long they will work with a particular piece of apparatus;
'formal' teaching—regular individual teaching sessions (short, say 10-20 minute, daily sessions would be the ideal, but longer, weekly or twice-weekly sessions will suffice with some children);

13

'informal' teaching—taking advantage of naturally occurring events and situations to 'reference' the goal words in the everyday setting; this means that other people coming into regular contact with the child (classroom assistants, members of the family) need to know what words are being taught: this is most simply done by having the words on a card fixed to the wall in the classroom or kitchen (or wherever you are most of the time with the child).

The four word categories

For purposes of teaching we have found it useful to divide the words up into four categories, the first three making up 90 per cent of the total. These word categories are as follows:

topics—the names of objects (including people and animals) which children use as topics of conversation when they do speak;

action words — words like 'walk', 'jump', 'up', 'down';
qualifiers — words like 'hot' and 'more';
personal-social — words such as 'hello' and 'oh dear'.

These last three categories usually form part of the first sentences — in combination with a topic word.

The three teaching levels

Teaching materials differ according to what kind of word you are teaching. But they also differ to some extent according to the *level* at which you are teaching, because when you start teaching a child the meaning of a word you will need to work at an easier level than you will later on. Very simply, the teaching process operates at three levels:

demonstrating — focusing the child on the word and what it refers to;
choosing — getting the child to show understanding of the word by making a choice, e.g. of one picture from two or three.
using — bringing the word into a conversation or improvised story involving dolls, models, puppets, and so on.

LEVEL ONE: DEMONSTRATING

To begin with words are demonstrated and talked round using those sorts of materials mentally handicapped children usually attend to: very large photographs, puppets, realistic models, colour slides in a viewer, photographs in a display cube, picture books, and so on. The aim is to bring into focus and 'shape up' the idea or *concept* giving meaning to the word.

This is achieved by presenting the same topic word or action word in a number of different ways and talking round it. So, for example, if 'car' is one of the words you want to demonstrate, you might have ready for the teaching session: a book with pictures of cars in it; a colour slide in a viewer; a large photograph of a car; a snap of your family car (together with pictures of other objects on a display cube); a couple of toy cars, and so on. By this means you can change materials quite quickly but keep attention on the topic whilst *you* talk about it. The aim is not to get the child to say 'car'—although he may produce the word spontaneously—but to get the 'car' concept related to the word. Remember that at this level in particular you are developing the child's *comprehension* of the word.

LEVEL TWO: CHOOSING

At this level the child has to *show understanding* of the words being taught but does not necessarily have to *say* them. Apparatus is used which involves the child in making a correct choice from two or three pictures or models ('Put the picture of the *clock* on here'). Psychologists call these *choice discrimination tasks* and they are the surest way of finding out whether a child really understands a particular word. But this approach does more than that: it makes him use the word *mentally* as part of a problem he has to think out, and this in turn encourages that level of *comprehension* which appears to be necessary for the development of independent speech. It seems to fix a word and its meaning in the child's mind so firmly that when he finds himself in a situation where it makes sense to use that word he can remember it without difficulty.

Children will quite often use the words independently at this level but even when they don't, if they show understanding by making the correct choices *they are still making progress in language.*

LEVEL THREE: USING

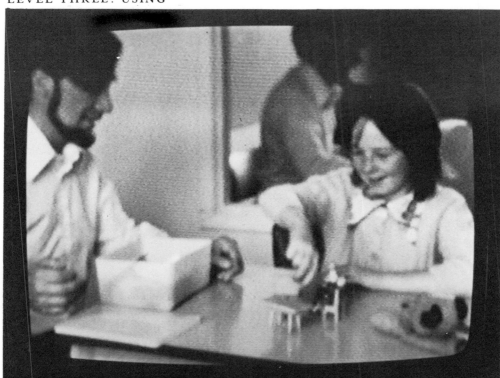

At a third level the words which have been taught in the fairly straightforward fashion described in Levels One and Two, are very deliberately worked into improvised stories using dolls, puppets and models. It is at this level that we find spontaneous speech sometimes 'drops into place' as the child sees where it can be fitted in. The child may say nothing (or very little) but if he is following your story then he is keeping track of what you say. The trick is to keep your running commentary going but to leave short gaps for the child to fit into. ('Now he's putting on his . . .' '*boots*'.)

Whilst some adults have a flair for the kind of improvisation required, with practice it is surprisingly easy for anyone to build up little stories and anecdotes round the goal words. Children differ in the style of approach they will accept — this is something that has to be explored — but the adult who is prepared to be unselfconscious and use 'funny' voices will not find it difficult.

How long is spent at any one level depends on the individual child. Some children need very little simple (Level One) referencing before they can go on to (Level Two) choice discrimination tasks. Teaching sessions involve 'testing the limits' of the child to see how far you can take him and going back if it is clear that he cannot cope.

You will find that a child will need to work mainly at one level, at least for a period of time — for example on choice discrimination tasks at Level Two. But new words always start at Level One no matter how quickly you move on. In part working at one level is due to the need to get the child used to the 'rules of the game' — what you are expecting of him. In a sense he has to *learn how to learn* — to see what the task involves as well as getting it right.

A difficult decision is judging when he is ready for another batch of 'goal' words. Some children quickly put the words they have comprehended into use in speech, but others need a longer 'incubation' period. In such a case you should move on to a new goal group to avoid becoming 'stale' or repetitive and then go back if the previous words are not appearing in speech. However, at this stage, when the word is not appearing in speech *even though good comprehension is definitely established* (as shown by the child's success on Level Two tasks), it is sensible to encourage the child to imitate the word. This may seem to be in flat contradiction of what I said earlier in the book; but there is a big difference between getting a child to repeat words he doesn't really understand and getting him to say a word when he has grasped the meaning. Saying the word is not the beginning but the end of the process, and some children may need a little prompting at this point — hearing *you* say the word and watching your lips as you do it.

The importance of individual teaching

You may wonder whether young mentally handicapped children can be expected to sit at a table and work with good concentration on a range of tasks. While this cannot be true for every child, in our experience it has been one of the real surprises. Obviously children's personalities and temperaments differ (as do those of their parents and teachers) and it is important not to gloss over this; but it is also important not to decide that deliberate teaching wouldn't work until you've really tried it out. The little girl shown working happily with her mother in the accompanying illustration is aged 2 years 3 months. One memorable experience was of a six-year-old boy with Down's Syndrome who, at a once weekly session, would willingly work for an hour and a half without flagging, and wept when the session was ended!

If the child enjoys the sessions and you feel you're getting somewhere then the 'formality' or the amount of time it takes is of no significance. But if the teaching sessions are a time of tension, bad temper and tears (other than those of pleasure) then they are positively harmful. With a little management, in most cases this situation need not arise.

The golden rule is to keep going for as long as the child's interest and attention can be maintained, and to stop quite firmly when he is clearly not co-operating. Most children find the materials and the individual attention desirable: they have to learn that to keep these they must co-operate. It is part of the learning-how-to-learn process.

Mentally handicapped children don't 'pick things up' incidentally to anything like the same extent that non-handicapped children do. What they need to learn has to be *brought to their attention* in a clear and compelling fashion—they can then often learn very well, and remember what they have learnt.

Individual teaching sessions are important because they provide a structured and focused setting: in a sense it makes more demands on the child than the everyday situation. In particular the child has to show a more precise understanding of word meanings. He can often get by with a good deal less than this in the day-to-day situation but the result is that he may not achieve as quickly as he might the level of comprehension needed for the effective production of words in speech. What I am suggesting is that there are two levels of comprehension: the sort of comprehension that is adequate for getting the general drift of what people are saying, and the sort of comprehension where the actual words and word meanings are going in *and staying there*. When a child has reached that point he is usually only a little way from effective, independent speech.

The importance of incidental or 'informal' teaching

This manual is mainly concerned with the 'formal' individual teaching sessions which are seen as central, but *on their own* they are unlikely to promote the useful development of language. If word meanings are to develop a broad base and a range of uses, the goal words also need incidental referencing in the natural everyday settings of home (and school).

The first essential is to have the current goal words firmly in mind—though it is a good idea to have a written list pinned up where it can easily be seen. Then you should think about the kind of situations and occasions which provide an opportunity to 'teach' incidentally—for example:

Goal Words	*'Natural' teaching situations*
Dog	—taking the child to see the next door neighbour's dog being fed.
Ball	—watching children playing football at the local recreation ground.
Hello	—always taking him to the front door to say 'hello' to callers.
Fish	—making a point of looking at fish on a fishmonger's slab and live fish in a pet shop.
Allgone	—always showing him empty bags and packets—particularly when he has taken things out or eaten things up.

It is possible to train yourself to be more self-conscious about using everyday events both out of doors as above, and in the home (like meals and bath-times), and you can also manipulate situations to make these opportunities arise more often than they might do otherwise, even if you do nothing more than draw the

child's attention to things. ('Look at the bubbles I'm making in the sink.') You will soon find that some 'natural' incidents hold a child's attention more than others—which guides your search.

The important thing is to reference words across a *variety* of uses and situations, extending this gradually so that the child can keep up with you. Just saying 'shoes' every time you put his shoes on may not do much for him. But, for example, if you can let him watch you cleaning shoes, and ask him to fetch his shoes to be cleaned, or show him his little shoe compared with his father's big shoe, or how you put your shoe on with a shoe horn, then you are more likely to gain his attention and get the *idea* of shoe across to him.

However, a note of caution is necessary here: by all means deliberately take advantage of language opportunities, but don't overdo it—there is no point in bombarding the child with language. It is the *quality* of the events (and their attention-holding power) that supports language development—not their quantity: too much may just be confusing.

Chapter 3

Getting Ready to Teach

The 'assessment for teaching' will have determined which words are going to be taught first—which are the 'goal' words. Just how many words to begin with depends on the probable rate of progress of the child concerned. For one child five goal words will seem ambitious, for another a dozen words may be needed to keep his interest.

The teaching materials described in the rest of this book are selected so that the goal words are presented to the child with as clear and 'concrete' a reference as possible, and in as many different ways as are feasible. The commercially produced materials are not expensive (with a few exceptions) and the 'home-made' apparatus is not difficult to make. Many special schools and local associations for the mentally handicapped have useful links with local secondary schools who are often very willing to make simple equipment in their workshops. Detailed plans and specifications for these 'home-made' items are provided in Appendix D.

Getting the materials together requires some discipline and effort: a range of materials is essential if the sessions are to be varied and interesting for the child. But it is not sufficient merely to have attractive materials. In addition it is necessary for whoever is doing the teaching (whether parent or 'professional') to have a firm grasp of the overall rationale—*why* the apparatus is being used in this way, to be well-organised in the individual teaching sessions, and to ensure that the words that are being taught are emphasised in everyday situations as explained in the previous chapter. If the child is of school age there should be close co-operation between home and school. Whether parent or teacher is responsible for the programmed teaching sessions, the other person needs to be kept informed of the current goal words in order to back up and reinforce the work that is being done. We have found that the special (ESN(S)) schools we have worked in normally maintain close contact with parents anyway so this is not perhaps as difficult as it sounds.

Daily sessions are not essential: three or four times a week is enough with occasional breaks for a week to avoid becoming stale. Sessions should last only as long as the child's attention can be held—perhaps just a few minutes to begin with.

The actual teaching sessions need to be well-defined for both the teacher and the child so that it is mutually recognised that specific activities are involved as part of a working relationship. A regular time of day helps to define this (preferably when the child is 'at his best'), so does individual attention—itself something to be worked for—and special, interesting apparatus which only appears on these occasions. We have found it useful to keep the materials that are currently being used in a medium-sized zip-round suitcase (the one in the accompanying illustration was bought from Marks and Spencer), but a large cardboard box does almost as well.

By this means the materials are always to hand and are not in danger of being mislaid. *It also ensures that they are kept as 'special' because they are not around all the time: we have found this to be very important.* If using the toys and apparatus is seen by the child as 'special' then he is more likely to be motivated to respond to the structure of the teaching sessions. To begin with the child has to learn the 'rules' of the game. Demonstration, a little free play, and trial runs using familiar materials (e.g. pictures or objects he already knows the names of) are usually sufficient. Once the use of the apparatus is established, the teaching of new word meanings can begin.

Within a session the goal words should be referenced in a number of different ways so different items (say, four or five) are introduced in order to sustain attention and interest at those moments when it appears to be slipping; but the *focus* of the session—the words that are being taught—remains constant.

No matter how free-wheeling the teaching session may be, if the teacher has clear aims and watches the child's responses then he (or she) will capitalise on the opportunities that arise—which should be many since the materials have been selected to support them.

Teaching should take place at a table with the child and adult facing each other and not too far apart. If a big table is used, this means sitting at right angles (like the mother and child in the illustration on page 19). Very suitable with small children is a low coffee table with the adult and child sitting opposite each other. The face-to-face element helps the adult to control the child's attention by watching where he is looking and observing how his mood and interest change. The table-top also provides a well-defined 'work space' which is important as part of the conventions of the programme sessions: either the child or the tutor (parent or teacher) can end the session by leaving the table. Thus, when the child is not co-operating, the tutor can clear up the apparatus saying 'Well, you don't want to do this now, we'll put the things away'; so the child who allows himself to be distracted away from the table finds that the special games (and the individual attention) are gone as a consequence. Needless to say they can reappear if he shows a real desire to work (and can disappear again, if necessary). This simple behaviour-modification approach with the games and individual attention contingent upon the child's co-operation is usually extremely effective.

The secret is to coax and manipulate the child but *never to pressurise him*. In our experience the commonest mistake is to try to keep the child working for too long—that is, after you have lost his attention and interest: at that point he is not learning anything—except that the materials and attention are there whether he concentrates or not. *If he is not co-operating, stop and put the things away*: it is no admission of failure to do so—failure is more likely to come through persisting with an unwilling child.

The four word categories and the three teaching levels

You will remember that we divided the different kinds of words in the basic vocabulary into four different categories—topics, action words, qualifiers and personal-social. The kinds of materials used to teach these words at the three levels of teaching—*demonstrating, choosing* and *using*—are described next.

Not all kinds of words can be taught at each level. You can't demonstrate in a simple (Level One) fashion personal-social words such as 'hello' and 'oh dear'; nor can you choose between them (Level Two); but they can easily be worked into an improvised story with model figures (Level Three). Similarly although you can demonstrate most of the words we call qualifiers, you can't choose between, for example, 'again' and 'cold'.

Only topic and action words can be taught at all three levels and action words present some problems. The topic words are of central importance—as their name implies. The topic words used by 20 per cent or more of the children in our first hundred words study are given in Appendix E together with similar lists of action words, qualifiers and personal-social words. We have used these lists as a basis for developing materials; *your* set of materials will be determined by the words you decide to teach.

Apparatus and teaching materials

FOR LEVEL ONE

Photographs and colour slides

Photographs and colour slides are a basic part of the programme and need to be of good quality. It is surprising how difficult it is to get suitable pictures of common objects. Pictures cut out of magazines are rarely adequate and even those from the large retail catalogues are a poor substitute for purpose-made pictures. In any case the cost is modest in terms of the results that can be obtained.

No standard list of pictures can cover completely the needs of individual children (the Polaroid 'instant' camera described later can help fill this gap) but we have developed a range of photographs and colour slides (different pictures of the same objects) which cover the topics in Appendix E and meet most requirements. It is possible these may be made available commercially but it is

perfectly feasible to make your own set. Since photographs soon become dog-eared it is better to mount them on card.

The colour slides are used in the hand viewer at Level One to focus attention: they are also used at Level Two. The small photographs are used at both levels in ways to be described.

Polaroid camera

This polaroid camera has been invaluable for producing *quickly* small pictures not in our collection. It is especially useful at the beginning stages of Level One and Level Two activities to obtain photographs of members of a child's family, a favourite toy and so on, but it can also be used to build up your own picture library.

(The camera illustrated is the basic 'Super Swinger' model costing around £7. The monochrome film (8 exposures) costs approximately £1.90; pictures taken indoors incur the additional cost of flash-bulbs.)

Large photographs

For children who are *just beginning* to develop an independent vocabulary, large photographs have demonstrated that it is possible to focus the attention of even very distractible children. At the Level One (simple referencing) stage different materials covering the same small goal vocabulary are essential to maintain attention and develop the concept underlying the word; large photographs add variety to the items in use but keep attention on the 'goal' words. The large photographs in the illustration are enlargements from the negatives used for our basic picture library. Their only disadvantage is the cost of producing them — privately or commercially: it is possible, however, that they could be made available through Toy Libraries and local associations for the mentally handicapped.

Line drawings

Although we know that children tend not to recognise line drawings of objects as easily as photographs or colour slides, they are useful for presenting objects in a different way, so helping to develop the object-concept. Drawings are also a means of getting pictures of things that are not easily photographed (like birds) or that don't occur very often in magazines.

Whilst you may not be much of an artist yourself, if you ask around you will almost certainly find that you know someone with a talent in this direction.

It is best to use a black felt-tip pen (or similar) then the drawings can easily be photocopied and so used many times and in different ways. In Appendix F you will find drawings of the fifty commonest 'topic' objects which you can photocopy for your own use. Photocopiers are normally available in public libraries, if you don't have access to one elsewhere.

Action photographs

These are large (7″ x 10″) black-and-white photographs, mounted on hardboard for durability, of a child (or children) sitting, running, standing, sleeping, jumping, etc.—intended to reference action words. They can be used in a (Level Two) choice discrimination game ('Where is the little boy sitting down?') or as a part of a performance to instruction game ('You stand up straight like that little boy').

Action slides and stick-man pictures

Referencing actions is not easy in static pictures—in many ways puppets (or humans!) are better because they can present the movement dimension. But pictures—if they are good ones—can 'fix' an action in a useful way.

One difficulty with photographs and colour slides, however, is that they may be seen more as a picture of a *person* than an *action*. Stick-man pictures (even those drawn by 'non-artists' as in the illustration opposite) get round this to some extent.

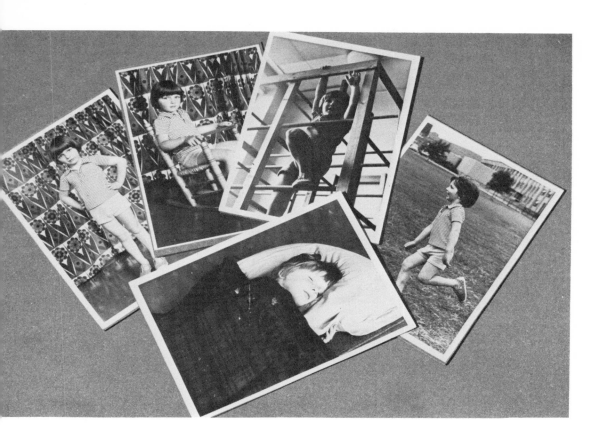

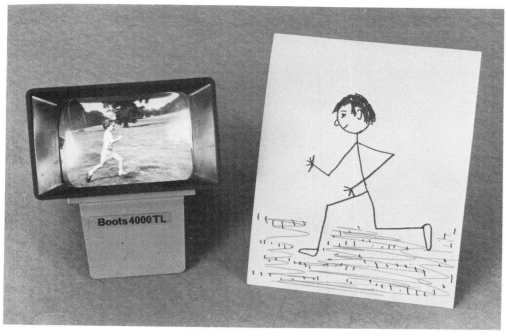

Picture frames

These frames—made out of vivid blue perspex—are designed to hold the photographs from our picture library. They have many uses—as one way of presenting pictures to talk about; as a (Level One) matching task (objects to pictures) which is excellent for developing the topic concept or category; and as a (Level Two) choice discrimination task (—'Show me the . . .').

Picture cube

The fascination—and attention-holding value—of picture cubes is obvious: whichever way you turn them a picture comes into view.

Commercially produced picture cubes are quite cheap but we have found that a wooden block, with a wooden insert-frame on each face, and painted in a bright colour is particularly effective. The photographs are held in place with Blu-tack.

Picture sticks boards

We originally designed these for use as choice discrimination tasks at Level Two. They were not very successful for that purpose but turned out to be a good way of presenting topic pictures (i.e. as an unusual way of looking at the pictures and talking about them).

The photographs are fixed on to the top of the sticks with a small piece of Blu-tack. Children find the activity of fitting the sticks in the holes and taking them out enjoyable in its own right and should be given the chance to do this to sustain motivation and attention, but not to the extent of distracting from the main task.

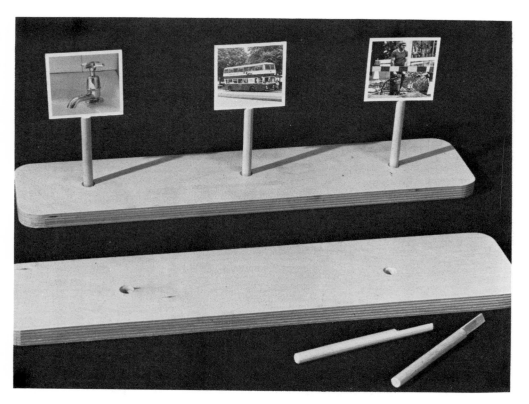

Scrap books and picture folders

Although magazines and retail catalogues are not as good a source of pictures as one might expect, within limits they are still useful. In particular they can provide lots of *different* pictures of some very common topics—like dogs, babies and cars.

Scrapbooks are cheap and easily obtainable. They can take pictures of all shapes and sizes; it is a good idea to have a page of small pictures of the same topic facing a page with one big picture, as in the illustration.

Display folders with slip-in polythene covers are usually obtainable only at photographic suppliers, stationers and stamp-dealers, and they are not as cheap (the large Rexel 'Nyrex' folder illustrated costs around £2.70). But their durability and versatility make up for that. Not only can you cut pictures out of magazines but you can also dismember picture-books to produce one suited to a particular child, and the pictures stay clean and undamaged.

The smaller display folders illustrated were bought from Boots (85p and 75p each): their advantage is that they are small enough to be easily handled by a child — whilst the pictures are safe! Although these can be used as part of the teaching sessions, *their main value is as a 'back-up' activity at some other time during the day*. Like the picture books on the next page they are best used to look at (and talk about) whilst sitting on the mother's or teacher's knee.

Picture books

Young mentally handicapped children often show great interest in picture books, especially when these are small enough for them to handle themselves.

There are a vast number of picture books available, but the contents are often not appropriate for the First Words Language Programme. Probably the best for our purposes, and the most easily available, are the Ladybird *Baby's First Book* and *Picture Books 1-5*; they cover many of the words on our basic list — this being especially true of *Baby's First Book* and *Picture Book 1* (illustrated below), although there is some overlap in the contents.

The books are best used not to cross-examine the child, or to engage in 'correct' naming exercises, but as a focus for talking round topic words during a teaching session, or as an enjoyable 'back-up' activity at some other time during the day.

Models of objects

These relate to the same list of words covered by the photographs and colour slides. It is rarely possible to make them satisfactorily (too small and too fiddly) and in any case moulded plastic models are cheap although not always very durable. Toy and model shops can supply most of the objects on our list but the fancy goods departments of some of the large chain stores (like Woolworths) are a source of models that are not readily available in toy shops. However, there are always some objects which are difficult to obtain in model form, although with some naturally small objects models are unnecessary.

We have found that the models need enough detail for easy recognition: this means that those models which consist of ambiguously shaped pieces of beechwood are unsuitable.

Apart from referencing topic words, models are valuable as part of a structured play situation, for example with small bendy dolls.

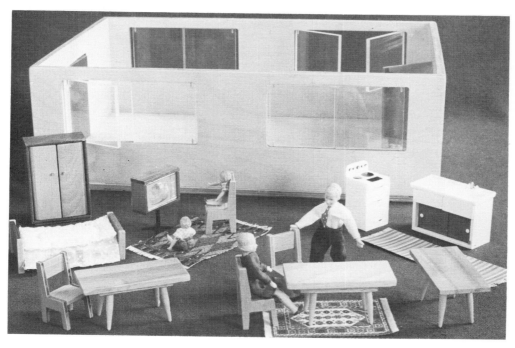

The basic room

The 'basic room' is designed to be readily adapted for use as a modern classroom, family living-room, kitchen or bedroom. It provides opportunities for the Level One referencing of a wide range of words but its main use is at Level Three, developing and using words. In particular it provides an opportunity for *structuring*, i.e. establishing the relationship between these words.

(The toy furniture and bendy dolls illustrated are manufactured or supplied by A. Barton & Co. [Toys] Ltd., New Addington, Surrey, except for the rugs and carpets [Lundby of Sweden].)

'Gone' box

This piece of apparatus is mainly used for referencing the word 'gone' — one of the most important action words in the vocabularies of young children and often forming part of their first sentences.

The apparatus is simple enough as the illustration makes clear, with a platform which can be 'dropped' by releasing a hook at the back. All manner of toys can be 'dropped' in this fashion and the action is very likely to encourage expressive use of the term on the part of the child, who can be asked to select 'victims' to be dropped, like little dolls or toy animals ('Dolly GONE!', 'Horse GONE!') which in turn helps to establish their identities.

 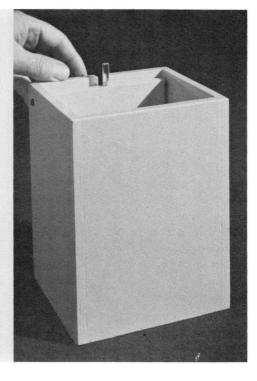

Action man

This well-known favourite toy of little boys has special virtues as a puppet being well-made with an articulated body (and gripping hands!) that can be fixed in different positions. This makes it possible to 'freeze' an action when referencing action words. As Action Men can be dressed and undressed they are sometimes more useful than conventional puppets for Level Three story telling.

The Action Man 'Adventurer' is the least military-looking model and there is a range of model equipment, some of it suitable for use in the programme.

(Action Men are made by Palitoy Ltd., Coalville, Leicester.)

Glove puppets and Pelham string puppets

Children are extremely variable in their response to puppets—some are indifferent, others treat them like small human beings. They can be remarkably effective in securing attention and stimulating the desire to communicate.

Puppets are versatile aids in teaching language: for example, asking the child to point to parts of the puppet's body (and then to the same parts on his own body), demonstrating action words, and (Level Three) storytelling involving words that have been worked on at the previous levels.

(The string puppet illustrated is manufactured by Pelham Puppets, Marlborough, Wiltshire, the glove puppet by Chad Valley Ltd.)

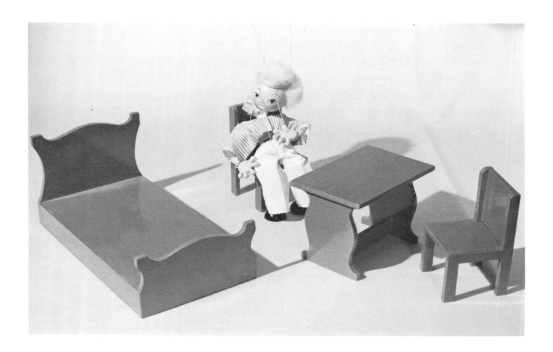

Puppet furniture

Since puppets have proved so versatile in use we have begun to design a range of puppet-sized models—to begin with, furniture. These are used for Level One referencing of action words and qualifiers such as 'on', 'up', 'sit down', as well as Level Three 'storytelling' using these goal words.

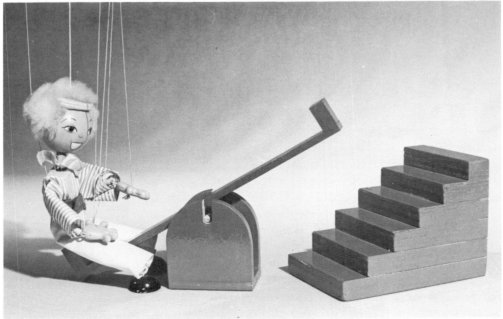

Stairs and seesaw

The use of these puppet-sized teaching aids is almost self-evident: to reference 'up' and 'down', although they can also be used to reference action words (e.g. 'jump'), or as part of a Level Three story ('Now he's going upstairs to bed') and so on. 'Stairs' and 'seesaw' both figure in the first hundred 'topic' words as well.

FOR LEVEL TWO

'Give me' games

The first 'choosing' games come out of the Level One activities, i.e. when you are putting the models away in the box saying 'give me the . . .' and so on. In other words it is part of the tidying up at the end of the session. But in doing this the principle of the child's making a choice according to your spoken instruction is being established and so leads in to Level Two activities.

The next 'choosing' game is the simple one of setting out a row of objects—two or three spaced well apart: this is more orderly than the 'tidying away' choosing and prepares the child for the other activities at this level.

For the youngest children (2-4 year olds) 'give me' games may be all they can manage at Level Two—but the Level Three storytelling is still important; this can be made to develop out of Level One 'talking around' by gradually extending its scope.

Viewer box

This is possibly the most successful single piece of equipment we have designed and since all of the other Level Two equipment serves a similar purpose it is worth describing the use of the 'Viewer Box' in some detail.

The child is asked to pick out one picture (of an object or an action) from two or three and put it on the sloping tray at the front of the box ('Put the picture of the dolly on here'). If the child makes the right choice then the teacher operates the slide viewer to show, very briefly, a slide of the same kind of object or action on the screen. The important thing to remember is that the screen does not light up until *after* the child has made the correct choice. In other words if he gets it right *something happens*. Making the screen light up is something that most children will work for, often with great enthusiasm.

This kind of task is important because it shows whether or not the child *really* understands the word. If he persistently makes a correct choice even though you vary the position of the card (or change the cards that go with it), then he has a firm hold of what the word refers to. We are fairly sure that when the child has reached this point of understanding, the word is potentially usable in *speech*.

Although the apparatus is simple, children have to learn how it works and what is expected of them. To begin with it is a good idea to use pictures (for example, of people the child knows) all of which he can pick out correctly. This makes it easier for him to grasp the rules of the game.

Later on when new words — that is words that have only been demonstrated at Level One — are brought in, it is best to use them initially with words that he has already shown he can pick out. This nudges the child in the direction of the correct choice and encourages the 'checking' strategy which is always necessary for success.

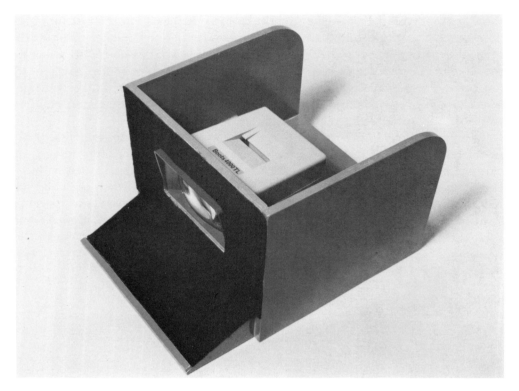

'Find it' box

This is used in the same way as the viewer box except that instead of a slide lighting up when the child makes a correct choice, he finds a model of the same object inside the box.

The front flap has a small knob on the box so that the child can lift it up to find the object. The swinging back of the box enables the teacher to remove the object if the child makes an incorrect picture choice.

Smartie boards

This apparatus was given its name because 'Smarties' have been used — hidden in the small hole underneath the picture or object — as the reward for picking up the right one ('It's under the duck', etc.). However, the real reward for most children is knowing they've got it right: one girl handed the sweets back to the teacher as she found them!

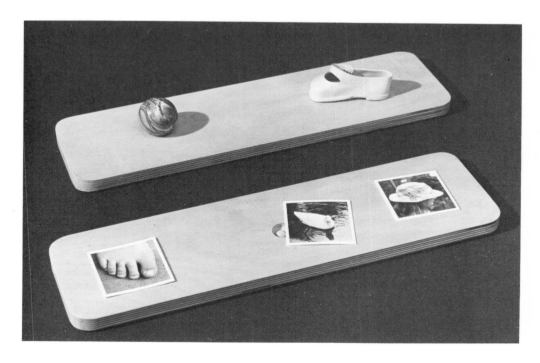

'Drop' box

This variant of the theme common to the other pieces of apparatus at Level Two is testimony to the unpredictable motivation of mentally handicapped children: one particular child would not work for anything else at this level.

The 'drop' is operated by the teacher releasing the catch at the back of the platform. The child has to pull the dummy lever at the front and if he selects the correct one ('Drop the chair!') then he has the satisfaction of seeing the object vanish from sight.

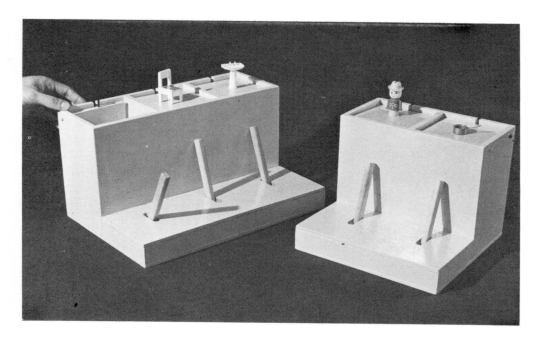

'Picture' boxes

This is a 'hide and find' game: the boxes are big enough to take a wide variety of objects which means you can select them to suit a particular child's interests.

The topic pictures which the child is learning to discriminate slip into the perspex lid on each box and can be changed quickly. The two-box version is used first. You start by naming the pictures on the lids and then demonstrate how you are going to hide something interesting in one of the boxes — drawing the child's attention to the picture on the lid. Then you show how if he listens carefully to what you say he can find what has been hidden right away (e.g. a bendy doll).

It is important to help the child to reflect on his choice — this is best achieved by having the boxes a little out of reach to begin with and moving them slowly within reach, repeating the word as you do so. If you don't do this the child will probably just lift up the lids at random, and since by this means he does eventually find the object, it is a difficult habit to break once established.

Level three play activities

Word meaning is not just a matter of labels correctly applied to objects or events — although correct labelling is an important thing for children to learn. Meaning ultimately depends on *use* — what words enable you to do in communicating with other people or in working things out in your head. When the child puts words into use in speech he also comes to learn something else — the way words can relate or link up with each other. To begin with the rules of grammar probably depend on the child perceiving how words he has learnt at a simpler level can be put together in practice.

It is fairly easy to specify the language teaching at Levels One and Two because they involve activities that are, to some extent, artificial and contrived — although useful for children who are not making normal progress in language. But we are aiming for *natural* language use and Level Three activities are intended as a bridge between the artificial and the real. These activities cannot be specified precisely for the simple reason that they need to be improvised.

The basic principle is straightforward: the 'goal' words which you have been concentrating on at Levels One and Two are worked into a conversation between a puppet, the teacher (parent) and the child, or into an improvised story using models (objects and human figures).

It takes some practice to become really fluent at this kind of invention but no-one with experience of children will find it difficult.

The aim is threefold:

—to bring in a number of different uses of the goal words—as part of a question, as a demand, a comment and so on, as well as repeating them several times;

> ('Where's the chair? Can you find the little chair? There it is. Give me the chair. Let's make the daddy sit down on the chair.'
> *'Mummy chair.'*
> 'Now the mummy's sitting on her chair.')

—to bring together those kinds of words that make up the first two-word sentences and most of which the child will have learnt in a simple way at Levels One and Two;

> ('Let's find the dolly's shoes. Are they in the bag? No, not there, the dolly's shoes have gone.'
> *'Shoes gone.'*
> 'Her shoes have gone. What will she do?')

—to give the child 'openings' where he might see the use of the words which are the focus of the session.

> ('First the mummy gives the daddy *his* dinner, then she gives the little girl *her* dinner, then she gives the little boy his . . .'
> *'Dinner.'*
> 'That's right. The little boy is going to have his dinner. What shall we give him for his dinner?' etc.)

Whilst it will be largely up to the teacher to keep things going it is important to make 'openings' for the child—a short pause or an unfinished sentence as in the above examples. Adjusting the level and pace of the story or conversation is something that can only be achieved intuitively. You will know when you have reached it because you will be holding the child's attention.

We have been very impressed by the responsiveness of mentally handicapped children to models and model-settings and by the impetus this gives to language once simple word meaning has been established. It may be because table-top play of this kind is itself, like language, *representational*—that is, it 'stands for' actual things and actual events. It is worth noting here that Piaget sees both 'pretend' (or 'symbolic') play and language, as manifestations of what he calls the 'symbolic function'—the ability to represent things mentally.

Conclusion

This manual has been completely rewritten twice and much of it has been revised many times. If the result looks tidy and straightforward it must be made clear that such tidiness is a fiction. In use and in practice everything—materials, teaching methods and so on—has to be modified. This is partly because individual children have their idiosyncrasies and partly because individual teachers have their own style. This personal dimension is something that cannot be written into a programme—it has to be added in. For this reason it was decided not to give verbatim transcriptions of teaching sessions (which we have on videotape) as had been originally intended.

You may ask whether *all* the apparatus we describe is necessary to carry out the full programme: the answer is *No*. You select (and invent) to suit a particular child; if you have any good ideas for apparatus we should like to hear about them. Attractive and 'special' materials are important (see the comments on page 23) but those described in this book can all be adapted to suit individual preferences and pockets. Even our simply-made apparatus can be made more simply (if less durably): we have made a satisfactory viewer box by cutting a hole in the side of a small cardboard box and supporting the viewer with two house bricks; the perspex picture frames can be made of hardboard and balsa wood spray-painted; a large tin can act as a 'gone box'—and so on. The *essence* of the programme is:

—the carefully structured step-by-step 'comprehension' approach to speech development;
—the selection of a goal vocabulary which is developmentally appropriate;
—the use of 'formal' and informal teaching;
—the emphasis on record keeping and evaluation so that a child's real progress can be charted and assessed.

By selecting, adapting and inventing materials and equipment the teacher or parent will in effect be making his (or her) own programme. Every child we have worked with has had a different programme 'package' which is why the evaluation procedure we have developed is for use with individual children. There is nothing miraculous about the approach we advocate or its effects: results are only achieved over time and through systematic hard work, and our experience has taught us to be cautious about what degree of success to expect with individual children.

Broadly speaking, we have found that the programme works best with Down's children but we have had successes with children whose mental handicap was due to unknown causes. What we are sure is that a systematic *structured* approach, provided it is used with sensitivity and imagination, is more likely to be effective than a vaguely 'stimulating' environment. This has certainly been true of the successful teaching we have observed in the ESN(S) schools that we have been working in during the past six years, and we would like to think of the present programme as an additional resource for parents and teachers of handicapped children, who are looking for realistic objectives.

Appendix A

Record Forms

Guide to record keeping

Usually imitated words and phrases come before independent words, and single words before the first two-word sentences. For this reason—and because they mark different stages in language development—three different kinds of record sheets are provided. These are:

'imitated' speech record—for imitated words or phrases;
'independent' word record—for single words that are not imitated;
sentence record—for two or three word 'sentences'.

You use these forms for your initial assessment; and as a record of progress once you have started teaching. The point at which you begin teaching each batch of goal words should be marked on each form.

Imitated speech

These are words and phrases the child speaks simply because someone else has just said them: they are usually repeated immediately, sometimes after a few minutes. For practical purposes we can say that if a word or phrase is repeated within five minutes it counts as an imitation.

Although imitated words are not so obviously important as the words a child speaks when he *means* something, it is still useful to know what words are imitated and *who spoke them in the first place*. You may also get important clues by knowing *what was going on at the time*. Finally (and this is particularly true of parents), since you know the child well, you may have some idea as to *why* he or she imitated that particular word. Since children quite often produce amongst their first independent words some they have previously imitated, it may be worth including a few of these words in the 'goal' vocabulary.

Independent words

It is not difficult to know when a child is saying a word because *he* has something to say. These words are of two kinds:

'proper' or 'public' words that almost anyone can understand, though they may not be very clear or complete (e.g. 'pop' for 'lollipop');
'private' words or 'family' words where the child knows what he means and so

do the people who know him, but a stranger probably wouldn't (e.g. 'duddy' for 'sweets').
Both kinds of words count.

Of course meaning doesn't just lie in the word: it depends *how* the child uses it and what *he* means by it. Parents and teachers can usually work out meanings better than someone who doesn't know the child very well. But in any case you can get closer to the child's meaning by asking: to whom was the word said? what was going on at the time? and what did the child seem to be communicating? — this is often more than one might expect from a single word. You also need to ask: was the word used again quite often?

All single words go on to the independent vocabulary record and also any *new* words that come in sentences.

Sentences

These usually come before a child reaches his first hundred words. And we find there are a few words (like 'gone' or 'more') that are combined with a lot of other different words. *Record each new combination* (e.g. 'cake gone', 'car gone' and so on), since this is an important measure of progress.

Sometimes it is difficult to work out whether what the child has said is really a two-word sentence or whether it's a case of two words made into one (a holophrase like 'allgone' or 'whassat?'). There is no sure way of knowing. The best rule is: if in doubt treat it as one word.

And remember to record any *new* words on the single word sheet.

'IMITATED' SPEECH RECORD

Word or phrase	Date first imitated	Who said the word or sentence that was imitated?	What was going on?	Why do you think he imitated what was said?

'INDEPENDENT' WORD RECORD

'Public' or 'private' word	Date first used	To whom (or to what) was the word said?	What was going on?	What do you think he was trying to say?	Was it used again fairly frequently?

SENTENCE RECORD

Sentence	Date first used	To whom or what used?	What was going on?	What do you think he was trying to say?	Was the sentence used again fairly frequently?

Reminder: List any <u>NEW</u> words in the sentence on the 'Independent' Word Record.

Imitated sentences go on the 'Imitated' Speech Record.

Appendix B

Theoretical Basis of the Programme

The principles of instruction on which this programme is organised are too well known to need exposition. What does need to be specified are the basic theoretical assumptions about the nature of early language: these are summarised here together with 'key' references.

1. That language, to begin with at least, 'maps on to' the concepts and categories which children have developed pre-language. This seems to be reflected in the kind of things children choose to talk about (Nelson, 1973; Thatcher, 1976) and the kind of categories apparent in the range of things children lump together in their use of single words (Clark, 1973).

2. That a certain level of cognitive development is a pre-requisite for the 'structured' use of language—whether these structures be sentences or single words used appropriately in the structure of real-life situations (Bloom, 1973; Sinclair, 1973; Halliday, 1975). It is significant that the rapid flowering of language in terms of vocabulary and sentence construction, occurs in normal children at around eighteen months, the point when they have reached the end of the sensori-motor stage of cognitive development (Piaget and Inhelder, 1969).

3. That the relation between language and cognition is particularly close at the beginning (single words to two-word sentences) stage, with this 'near-match' acting as a 'priming' function for the language 'engine' which quickly develops a more independent, self-functioning role (Schlesinger, 1971; Cromer, 1974).

4. That comprehension in some degree necessarily precedes the development of independent purposive speech (Ingram, 1974).

References

Bloom, L. 1973. *One Word at a Time*. The Hague: Mouton.
Clark, E. V. 1973. 'What's in a word? On the child's acquisition of semantics in his first language.' In T. E. Moore (ed.) *Cognitive Development and the Acquisition of Language*. New York: Academic Press.
Cromer, R. 1974. 'The development of language and cognition: the cognition hypothesis.' In B. Foss (ed.) *New Perspectives in Child Development*. Harmondsworth: Penguin Books.
Halliday, M. A. K. 1975. *Learning How to Mean*. London: Arnold.
Ingram, D. 1974. 'The relationship between comprehension and production.' In R. L. Schiefelbusch and L. L. Lloyd (eds.) *Language Perspectives: Acquisition, Retardation and Intervention*. London: Macmillan.

Nelson, K. 1973. 'Structure and strategy in learning to talk.' *Monographs of the Society for Research in Child Development 38*, (1-2, Serial No. 149).

Piaget, J. and Inhelder, B. 1969. *The Psychology of the Child*. London: Routledge and Kegan Paul.

Schlesinger, I. M. 1971. 'Production of utterances and language acquisition.' In D. I. Slobin (ed.) *The Ontogenesis of Grammar*. New York: Academic Press.

Sinclair, H. 1973. 'Language acquisition and cognitive development.' In T. E. Moore (ed.) *Cognitive Development and the Acquisition of Language*. New York: Academic Press.

Thatcher, J. W. 1976. 'An analysis of the structure, function and content of the beginning vocabularies of babies: the first hundred words.' *Unpublished MA dissertation:* University of Nottingham.

Appendix C

Evaluation Technique

Selecting goal and control words

To take an actual example, John (aged seven years) had thirteen independent words before teaching started. Goal and control words were taken from Stage Two of the developmental lists. Excluding words that John had already, ten pairs of words were selected: these are shown below together with the result of tossing a coin for each pair. You will see that as far as possible similar words have been paired.

1.	dog	duck (heads)
2.	horse	shoe (tails)
3.	book	ball (tails)
4.	bird	baby (tails)
5.	down	bye-bye (heads)
6.	teddy	clock (tails)
7.	teeth	ear (heads)
8.	cup	bag (heads)
9.	tree	flower (heads)
10.	fish	cow (tails)

Tossing the coin decides which word in each pair will be taught: if heads come up it is the first word in the pair, if tails come up then it is the second one. The point of doing this is to ensure that words are assigned randomly to each group, otherwise it would be tempting to choose as goal words those that are likely to be learnt more easily than the control words.

Next we have the twenty words divided into a 'goal' group and a 'control' group.

Goal group	Control group	
*dog	duck	+
*shoe	horse	+
*ball	book	+
*baby	bird	+
down	bye-bye	=
*clock	teddy	+
teeth	ear	=

58

cup	bag	=
*tree	flower	+
cow	fish	=

The words starred are the ones subsequently produced in speech during the following four months. All the pairs have a + or = sign against them; no control words appeared in speech but, as one would expect, three extra words were produced that had not been deliberately taught ('bubbles', 'chair' and 'mine'). The signs are employed as follows:

a *plus* sign (+) indicates that the goal word appeared but the control word didn't;

a *minus* sign (−) indicates that the control word appeared but the goal word didn't (which didn't happen in this example so there are no minus signs);

an *equals* sign (=) indicates that both words appeared (or didn't appear) in speech.

We have a total number (N) of ten pairs. We reduce the size of N by the number of pairs that are 'equal' (=). There are four of these equal pairs so N is reduced to six. We call the number of minus signs 'x'; since there are none of these (although there might have been) $x = 0$. With these two values ($N = 6$ and $x = 0$) we are able to use an appropriate table of probability. From this we can read off the probability of the obtained result being due to chance. Here the probability is .016, or about 1 chance in 60, so we can be reasonably certain that our teaching in this instance was effective.

To keep the illustration simple we have chosen an example where not many pairs are involved but the results are very clearcut. This is not likely to be so in every case and it is usually more sensible to wait until twenty or thirty words have been taught before carrying out the evaluation — or even to wait until you have gone as far as you intend going.

The test of significance used in this example is called the Sign Test and is fully described on pages 68-75 of: Siegel, S. 1956. *Nonparametric Statistics for the Behavioral Sciences.* New York: McGraw-Hill. An appropriate table for the calculation of probabilities is given on page 250 of the same book.

Full details of the formal evaluation of the programme can be obtained by writing to the author at the Child Development Research Unit, University of Nottingham.

Appendix D

Plans for Making Apparatus

Note: Metric measures are given for *thickness* of plywood, hardboard and perspex because this is how they are now sold; otherwise imperial measures are used.

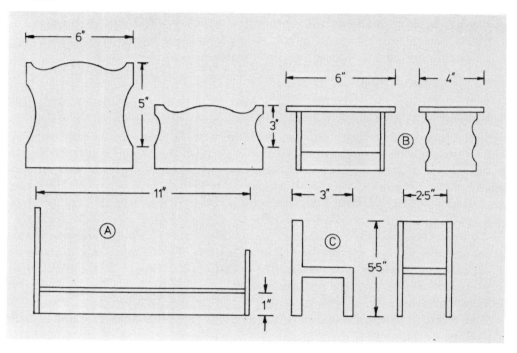

Puppet furniture

1. Cut the bed ends 6″ x 6″ x 6mm and 6″ x 4″ x 6mm ply. These may be left square or shaped as shown.
2. Cut the base for the bed 11″ x 6″ x 6mm and the side strips 11″ x 1″ x 6mm.
3. Clean, glue and pin together.
4. Cut the table top 6″ x 4″ x 6mm.
5. Cut the table ends 4″ x 3¼″ x 6mm. Again these may be left square or shaped.
6. Cut the bottom stave 4½″ x 1″ x 6mm.
7. Clean, glue and pin together.
8. Cut the chair sides 5½″ x 3″ x 6mm. The legs are 2½″ long by ½″ wide.

60

9. Cut the chair back and seat. These are both 2¾" x 2½" x 6mm.
10. Clean, glue and pin together.

The bed, table and chairs were painted red.

Stairs and seesaw

Seesaw
1. Cut the plank 12" x 1" x 6mm ply.
2. Cut the seat ends 1" x 1" x ½".
3. Cut the pivot block 1" x 1" x ¾" and drill a hole ¼" diameter through the centre.
4. Cut a piece of ¼" dowel 2" long.
5. Glue and pin together as in the drawing.
6. The support frame is made from 9mm ply. Cut two pieces 3" square and one piece 3" x 2".
7. Round the tops of the side boards as shown and cut the pivot slots ¾" deep by $\frac{5}{16}$"wide.
8. Glue and pin the sides onto the base.

Stairs
1. Make the stairs from a strip of 19mm ply 4" wide.
2. Cut lengths from the strip 6"−5"−4"−3"−2"−and 1".
3. Glue and pin together as in the drawing.

The seesaw and the stairs were painted red.

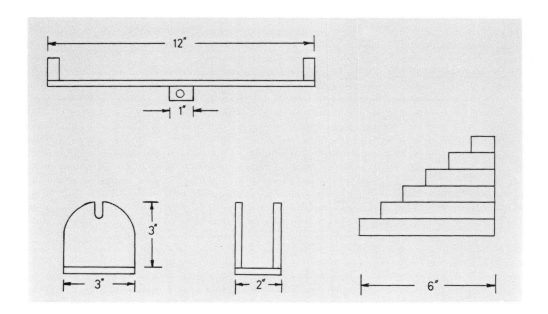

Basic room

1. Cut window sides 18″ x 5½″ x 6mm ply.
2. Cut door sides 12″ x 5½″ x 6mm ply.
3. Cut floor 18″-x 12½″ x 9mm ply.
4. Cut out for windows 6″ x 3″.
5. Cut out for door 4½″ x 3″.
6. Cut windows from 3mm clear perspex and door from 3mm coloured perspex. Allow for ⅛″ clearance all round.
7. Drill holes from the top edge of both window and door sides for pin hinges. These holes are drilled ¼″ from the edge of the window and door cut-outs.
8. Drill holes for pin hinges in the doors and windows (C). These are drilled ⅛″ from the edge and ¼″ deep.
9. Fit door and windows by putting a ½″ panel pin in the bottom hinge hole and place in position. This puts the window flush with the top of the cut-out. The ⅛″ clearance is made by driving in the top hinge pin.
10. Glue, pin and finish the complete room.

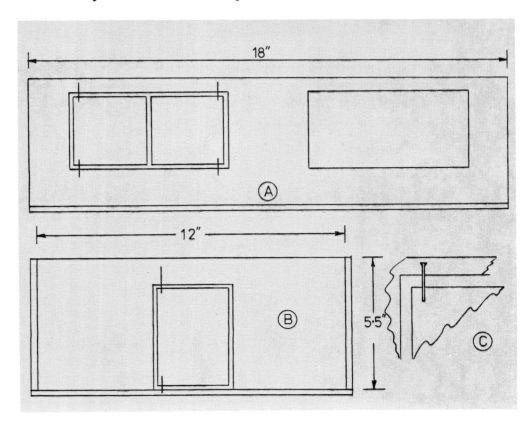

Picture sticks and Smartie boards

1. Cut the peg board from 19mm ply 18″ x 4″ (B).
2. Drill ⅜″ holes all the way through; in one board the two holes are on 9″ centres, and in the other board the three holes are on 6″ centres.
3. The 5″ x ⅜″ diameter pegs are cut 5″ long and as in the drawing.

1. The Smartie boards are cut as for the peg boards but are 5″ wide (A).
2. The holes are drilled on the same centres as for the peg boards but are ⅞″ diameter and ¼″ deep.
3. The base of the boards is covered with green felt.

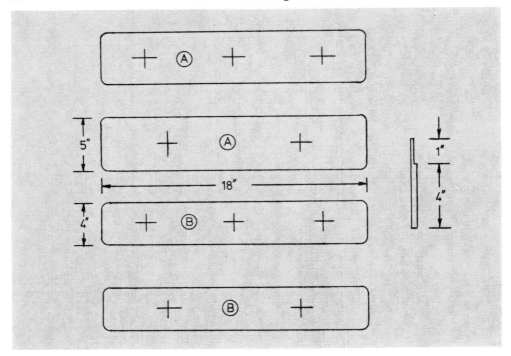

Picture frame boards and picture cube

1. Cut the base boards from 3mm blue perspex; the single boards are 3¼″ wide.
2. Cut the picture support strips; the edge strips are ½″ wide and the centre strips are 1″ wide.
3. Cut the strips to suit the pictures, picture size, 2¾″ square and glue into position.
4. Round the corners.

    These boards can be made just as easily from thin plywood.

The picture cube is made from hardwood. The cut-outs for the photographs can be made either by milling them out or by gluing on ½″ x ⅛″ strips.

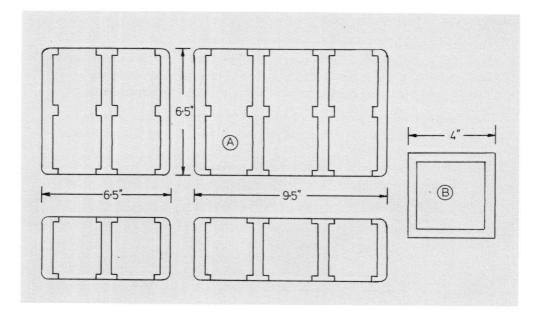

1. Cut the two sides 8″ x 8″ x 9mm and radius one corner.
2. Cut the floor 8″ x 8″ x 9mm.
3. Cut the front panel 8″ x 6″ x 9mm and cut out the hole for the slide-viewer. If the Boots 4000TL model is used this hole should be 4½″ x 2¾″, and 1⅛″ from the bottom.
4. Glue and pin the sides, floor and front to the base.
5. Cut two viewer mountings 8″ x 1⅜″ x 19mm ply. The front mounting should be cut as in (C) to a depth of ½″.
6. Fit the mountings, the front one should be flush to the front panel and the rear one 3¼″ further back.
7. Sand and paint.
8. The bottom should be fitted with rubber feet.
9. The front panel and photograph support should be painted matt black.

Base for the Viewer box and the Find it box

This base is used for both the Viewer box and the Find it box.

1. Cut two lengths of 2″ x 1″ planed deal 11½″ long.
2. Cut three lengths of 2″ x 2″ planed deal 6¼″ long.
3. Glue and pin together as in (A).
4. Cut off and plane part (C).
5. Cut, glue and pin 8″ x ⅜″ x 9mm ply photograph support.
6. Sand and square.

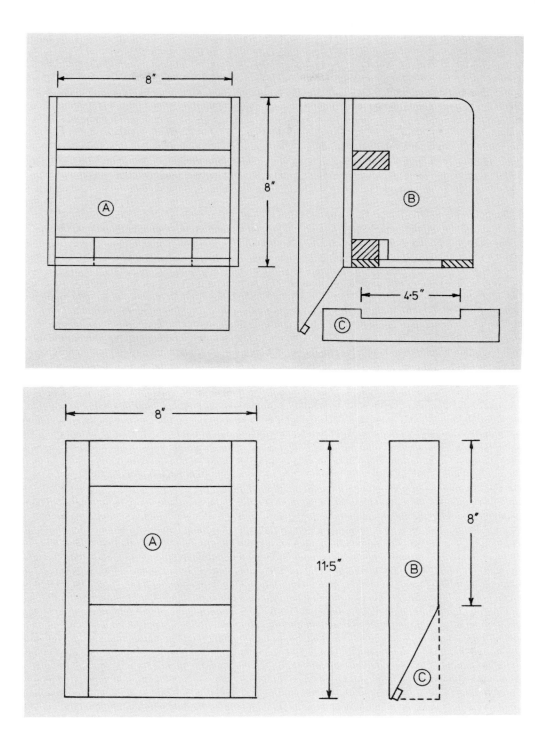

Find it box

1. Cut the sides, two pieces 8″ x 8″ x 9mm ply, and drill for the pin hinges. The holes should be slightly smaller than the pins, ¼″ from the top and ⅛″ from the sides.
2. Cut the box top 8¾″ x 7¼″ x 9mm ply.
3. Cut the floor of the box 8″ x 8″ x 3mm hardboard.
4. Glue and pin the sides to the base.
5. Glue and pin the top.
6. Cut the front door stops ⅜″ square x 7⅜″, glue and pin in place.
7. Sand and paint.
8. Cut perspex doors 7⅞″ x 5⅞″ x 3mm coloured perspex and drill for hinge pins ¼″ from the top (C) and use a drill slightly larger than the pins.
9. Drill and fit a knob to the front door.
10. Fit both doors. The panel pins used for the hinges should reach the bottom of the holes in the perspex when the pins have been punched below the surface of the wood (C). The punch holes should be filled with a stopping.
11. Fit rubber feet.

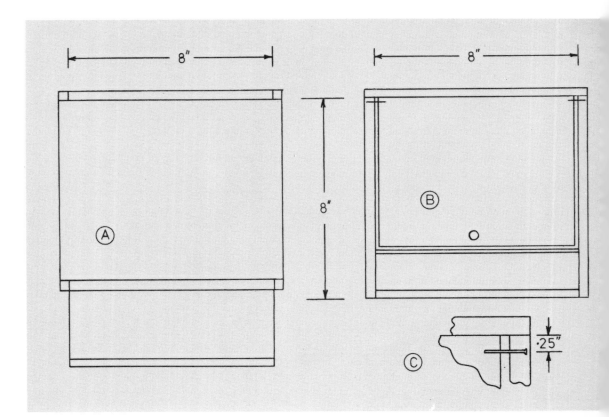

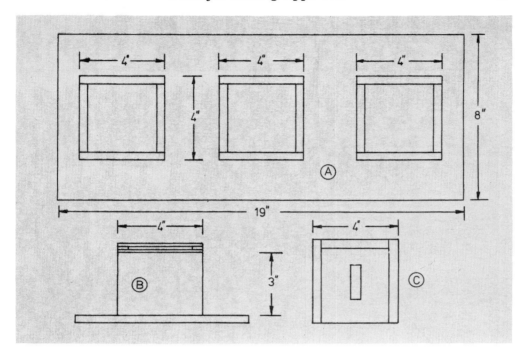

Picture boxes

1. Cut box sides from 9mm ply to make boxes 4″ square by 3″ high.
2. Glue and pin the boxes together.
3. Cut the base boards 14″ x 8″ x 9mm for the two box model, and 19″ x 8″ x 9mm for the three box.
4. Glue and pin the boxes to the base board leaving equal spaces.
5. Cut the lids from 3mm perspex, two 4″ squares, one 4″ x ½″ strip and two 3½″ x ½″ strips for each lid. The bottom square of each lid should be of coloured perspex and have a 2″ x ½″ slot to allow the removal of the photograph. Between the bottom square and the top square (clear perspex) the ½″ strips are inserted to allow the picture to slide in.
6. Glue the lid pieces together.
7. Clean and paint the boxes and fit rubber feet.

Gone box and drop box

1. Cut the main box sides 15″ x 8″ x 9mm ply.
2. Cut the main box ends and partitions 8″ x 4¼″ x 9mm ply.
3. Cut the catch slots in the back 1″ x $\frac{5}{16}$″ as in (D).
4. Drill $\frac{3}{16}$″ holes for hinge screws in the ends and partitions, ½″ from the top and ½″ from the side.
5. Glue and pin the box together.

6. Cut the box lids 4¼" x 4" x 9mm and drill ⅛" holes for the hinges $\frac{5}{16}$" from one end and ⅜" deep.
7. Cut the base board 15" x 10" x 6mm ply and the front lever supports one piece 15" x 5" x 6mm, two pieces 15" x 1¼" x 6mm and two pieces 4½" x 1¼" x 6mm.
8. Cut lever slots in the lever top board 1½".
9. The lever hinge (C) is made from a 2" piece of 2" x 1" planed and the hinge itself a 1½" panel pin. The lever is cut 5" x ⅞" x ⅜".
10. Glue and pin the lever under the top board with the lever central in the slot.
11. Complete the total assembly but for the lids.
12. Finish and paint.
13. Fit the lids; the centre hinges are ⅛" pegs ⅞" long and the end hinges are eight round-headed screws ¾" long.
14. Drill and fit the catch pegs in the lids (D) and fit catches.
15. Fit rubber feet.

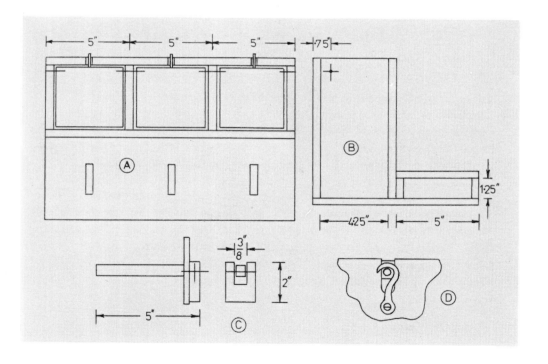

Appendix E

Word Frequency Lists

TOPIC WORDS: FREQUENCY

91-100%
(Person's name—friends and members of the family)
Baby Ball *Bird Book Daddy *Clock Car *Dog Mummy Shoe *Teddy

81-90%
Bath Door

71-80%
Biscuit Eye Horse Spoon

61-70%
Bike Boat Bus *Cow *Cat *Drink Nose Tree Toe Tea

51-60%
Button Ear Fish Key(s) Teeth Train Toast

41-50%
Bubble Brick Bed Bunny (rabbit) Banana Bag Balloon
Brush Chair Cake Cheese Coat Duck Hair Hat Hand
House Juice Knee Light Milk Pin Pea Paper Socks Seesaw

31-40%
Dolly Dinner Egg Flower(s) Fork Fly (Flies) Lorry
Milkman Mouse Plane Peg Purse Stairs Scissors
Tap Tractor Water

21-30%
Apple Boy Bridge Boot Bib Bowl Blanket Bread Chocolate
Cup Drawer Gate Garden Goose Lollipop Meat Man Moon Mouth
Orange Pudding Potatoes Potty Pram Pen Pear Soap Swing
Spade Shirt Towel Van

There are just over one hundred words on this list. We have used it as the basis for developing a picture library (photographs and colour slides) and model object library. Those starred (*) were spoken in a variety of different ways, almost always the obvious ones (like 'doggie' and 'bow-wow') but most children had a few idiosyncratic names for things, like the little girl who called trains 'whoosh'.

69

TOPIC WORDS: ALPHABETICAL ORDER

Apple	Cat	Hand	Pin
Baby	Chair	Hat	Potatoes
Bag	Cheese	Horse	Potty
Ball	Chocolate	House	Pram
Balloon	Clock	Juice	Pudding
Banana	Coat	Key(s)	Purse
Bath	Cow	Knee	Scissors
Bed	Cup	Light	Seesaw
Bike	Daddy	Lollipop	Shirt
Bin	Dinner	Lorry	Shoe
Bird	Dog	Man	Soap
Biscuit	Dolly	Meat	Socks
Blanket	Door	Milk	Spade
Boat	Drawer	Milkman	Spoon
Book	Drink	Moon	Stairs
Bowl	Duck	Mouse	Swing
Boy	Ear	Mouth	Tap
Bread	Egg	Mummy	Tea
Brick	Eye	Nose	Teeth
Bridge	Fish	Orange	Teddy
Brush	Flower(s)	Paper	Toe
Bubble	Fly (Flies)	Pea(s)	Toast
Bunny	Fork	Pear	Tractor
Bus	Garden	Peg	Train
Button	Gate	Pen	Tree
Cake	Goose	(Person's Name)	Van
Car	Hair	Plane	Water

TOPIC WORDS: CATEGORIES

FOOD, etc.
Apple Biscuit Banana Bread Cake Cheese Chocolate Drink Dinner
Egg Juice Lollipop Milk Meat Orange Pea(s) Pudding Potatoes
Pear Tea Toast

PEOPLE
Baby Boy Daddy Mummy Milkman Man (Person's name—friends
and members of the family)

ANIMALS
Bird Bunny Cow Cat Dog Duck Fish Fly (Flies) Goose Horse
Mouse

VEHICLES, etc.
Boat Bike Bus Car Lorry Plane Train Tractor Van

BODY PARTS
Eye Ear Hair Hand Knee Mouth Nose Toe Teeth
CLOTHING
Button Coat Hat Shoe Socks Shirt
HOUSEHOLD ITEMS, etc.
Bag Bath Bed Bin Brush Bowl Blanket Clock Chair Cup Door
Drawer Fork House Key Light Pin Paper Peg Purse Potty Pram
Pen Spoon Stairs Scissors Soap Tap Water
GARDEN AND 'OUTSIDE' THINGS
Bridge Flower Gate Garden Moon Seesaw Swing Spade Tree
TOYS
Ball Book Bubble Brick Balloon Dolly Teddy

ACTION WORDS: FREQUENCY

91-100%
—

81-90%
—

71-80%
Down Gone

61-70%
Bang

51-60%
—

41-50%
Sit (down) Up Walk

31-40%
Allgone Come

21-30%
Carry Go Jump Kick Splash Shut

QUALIFIERS: FREQUENCY

91-100%
—

81-90%
—

71-80%
—

61-70%
Hot More Where

51-60%
—

41-50%
Again   Outside   There
31-40%
Dirty   My
21-30%
Bad   Big   Cold   Mine   Nice   On   Wet

PERSONAL-SOCIAL WORDS: FREQUENCY

91-100%
Bye-bye
81-90%
—

71-80%
Hello
61-70%
No
51-60%
Oh dear
41-50%
Ta
31-40%
Here y'are   Look   Me   Please
21-30%
Night-night   Peep bo   Thank you   What's that (whassat, etc.)   Yes

DO MENTALLY HANDICAPPED CHILDREN USE THE SAME
WORDS AS NON-HANDICAPPED CHILDREN?

The 'goal' words in the language programme are based on our study of vocabulary development in fourteen non-handicapped children. If handicapped children could be shown to use a *different* set of words then we might be wrong in using this 'normal' data. For this reason we carried out a comparative study following up four Down's children from the time they started to talk. As expected, we found that they wanted to talk about the same things as 'normal' children and in the same way—but progress was slower and they used language less often. To illustrate this we give below some of our findings. First, a comparison of the content of the first ten words produced, and secondly a comparison of the 'high frequency' topic words.

FIRST TEN WORDS (of all kinds)

The most frequent words are given first.

Non-handicapped group

Daddy	No	Tea	Bear
Mummy	Bird	Get down	Bath
Car	Biscuit	Bang	Duck
(Person's name)	Tree	Lamb	Clock
Dog	Shoe	Juice	Sh sh
Teddy	Horse	Bubbles	Lion
Baby	There	Nose	Fish
Cat	Hello	Button	Light
Bye-bye	Sock	Toe	Hot
Ta	Banana	Brush	Good girl
Gone	'Tis it?	Burn	Key
(Drink)	Bus	Dinner	Owl
Ball	Spoon	Boo	

Handicapped group

(Person's name)	Book	Egg	Mine
No	*Dog*	Eye(s)	*Baby*
Cat	More	*Car*	*Down*
Mummy	Knickers	Ear(s)	*Boo*
Daddy	Sweets	Yes	Door
Ta	*Clock*	Look	*Teddy*
Hair	Apple	*Hot*	Kick

The words italicised also occur in the first ten words of the non-handicapped group; there are more words in the first group mainly because there were more children in it.

The handicapped children were not amongst those we were teaching.

'HIGH FREQUENCY' (50% +) TOPIC WORDS USED BY CHILDREN
IN THE HANDICAPPED GROUP

(Person's name)	Ear(s)	Ball	Duck
Dog	Hair	Bike	Key
Mummy	Cake	Book	Plane
Cat	Bed	Cow	Sweets
Dad	Bell	Clock	Shoe
Eye(s)	Baby	Dinner	

The words italicised were also amongst the 'high frequency' (50% +) topics for
non-handicapped children.

Topic Drawings to Photocopy

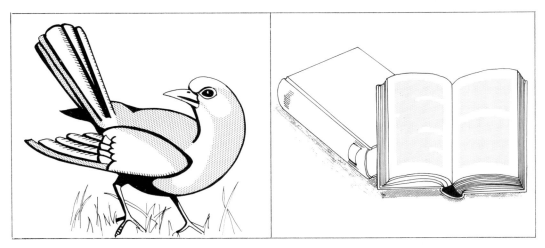

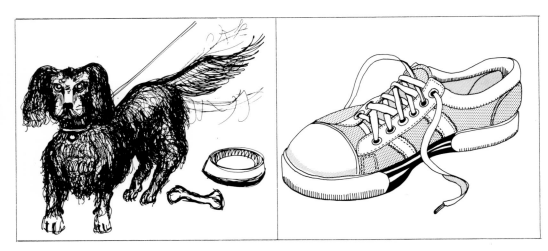

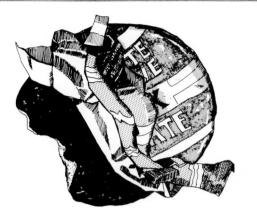

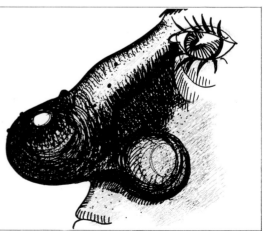

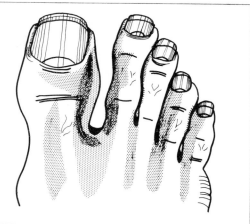

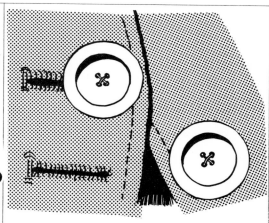
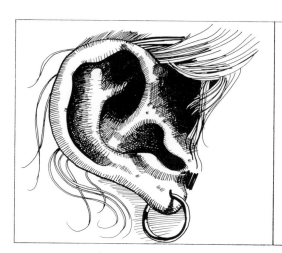

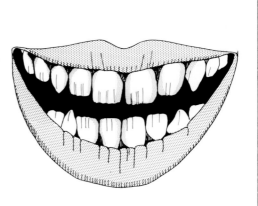

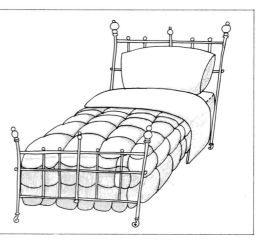

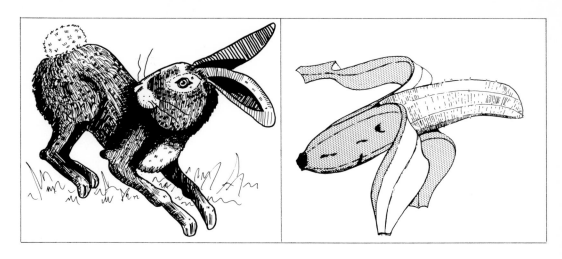

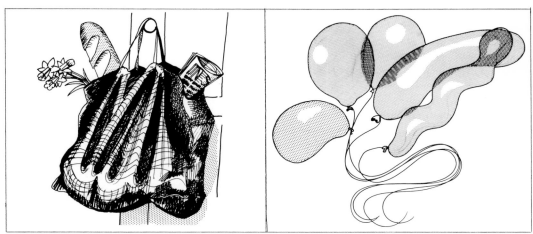

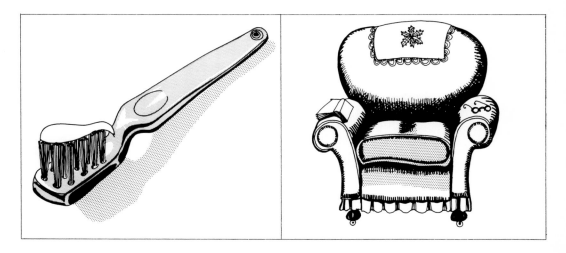

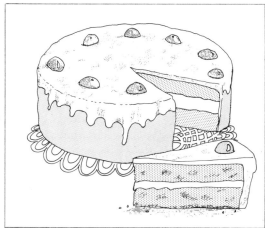
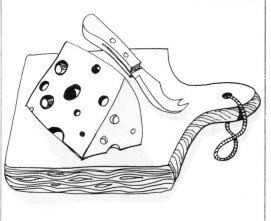

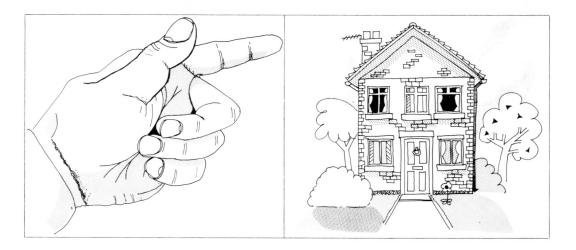

The drawings in this appendix are copyright but are provided for you to photocopy for use with the child you are teaching. Reproduction for any other purpose must only be with the permission of the publisher.